The love in my body and heart
For the earth's shadow and light
Has stayed over years.

With its cares and its hope it has thrown
A language of its own
Into blue skies.

It lives in my joys and glooms
In the spring night's buds and blooms
Like a Rakhi-band
On Future's hand.

A poem by Rabindranath Tagore

In memory of my Grandmother, Girija,
and her brothers; Gauri, Uma and Chottan.

anJana
publishing limited

March 2021

L, Orient Crest,
76 Peak Road, The Peak, Hong Kong

ISBN: 978-988-79059-8-1

Designed by Jump Web Services Ltd
Printed at Thomson Press India Ltd.

Amma, Tell Me About

Raksha Bandhan!

Illustrated by
Maulshree
Somani

Written by
Bhakti
Mathur

The boys stared wide-eyed at the
Countless colourful rakhis on display.
"Look Krishna, and Hanuman!" pointed Kiki,
"Amma, I'd like to wear a rakhi every day!"

It was the evening before Raksha Bandhan;
Amma had taken Klaka and Kiki to the bazaar.
They had come to buy gifts for their cousin Maya:
One bought a picture book, the other a candy jar.

They both awoke early the next day.
For once, they were ready on time!
They helped wrap the gifts for Maya
And waited for the doorbell to chime.

It wasn't a long wait: Maya soon arrived.
She was shy at first and hid behind her mother.
Some smiles and a hug brought her out, and soon
They were laughing, playing, chasing one another.

The three started off on a rowdy game of tag;

Their shouts almost brought the house down.

Till Amma said, "Maya, it's time for you

To tie rakhis to this joker and that clown!"

Maya's mom handed her a beautiful silver plate -
Loaded with laddus, a diya and kumkum powder.
Kiki bounced on the sofa and Klaka said excitedly,
"The rakhis we wanted!" his voice getting louder.

Maya put a red tilak on their foreheads
And tied a rakhi to each eager boy's wrist:
Brave Hanuman for Kiki, clever Krishna for Klaka.
They then ate the laddus. They were hard to resist!

The boys gave Maya the gifts they had got for her.
She was thrilled, hugging one and then the other.
"Amma, tell us about Raksha Bandhan!" said Klaka,
"And why does a sister tie a rakhi to her brother?"

"Well, the word 'Raksha' means to protect and
'Bandhan' means a bond of love," Amma said.
"It is a promise to love and protect each other,
Sealed by the tying of rakhi's special thread.

Yes, sisters tie rakhis to brothers, but then
You can tie a rakhi to anyone you want to,
Like a friendship band, this string can be tied:
To a sibling, a cousin, a friend, a parent too.

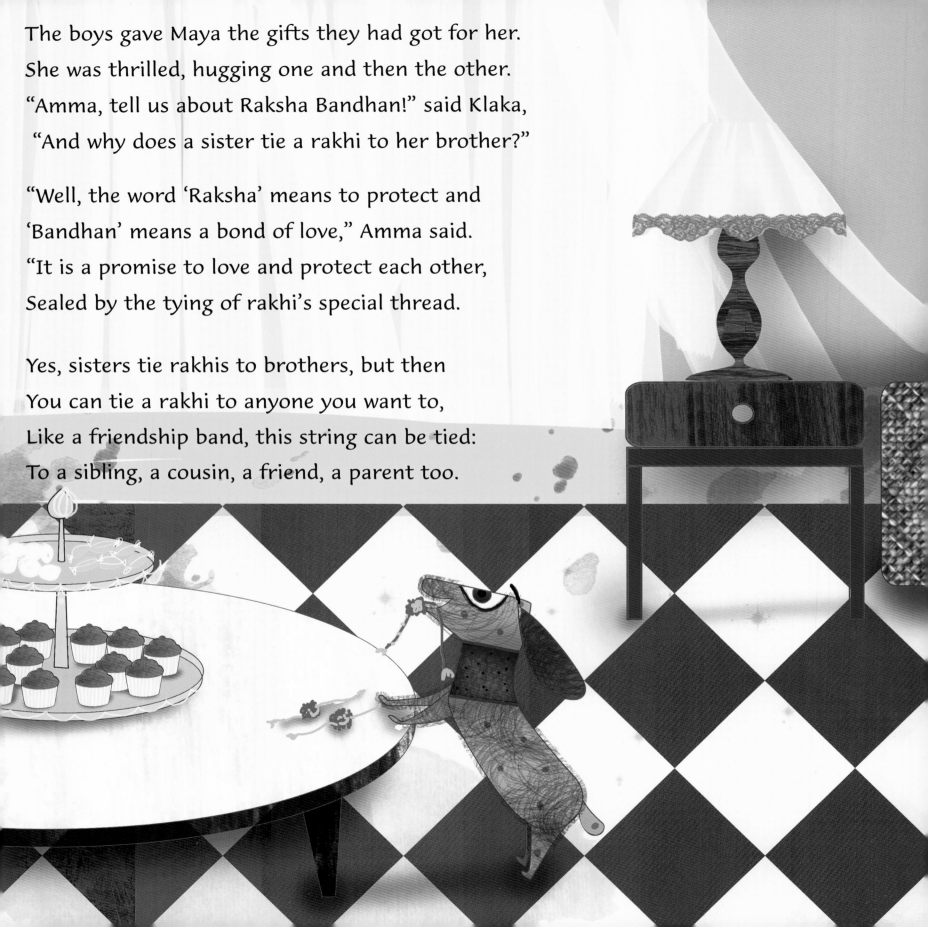

There are tales galore about Raksha Bandhan.
Let me begin with the story of Bali, a famous king:
He possessed all that a person could desire,
And yet he was not very happy with anything.

With a burning ambition to rule the world,
He set off on his chariot, mighty army in tow.
Conquering land after land, flung far and wide,
Seemingly intent on spreading terror and woe.

Lord Vishnu, upon hearing of Bali's atrocities,
Was enraged and said: "Bali is a disgrace,
Such tales I had heard about his generosity,
Now it seems he needs to be put in his place!"

The next day as Bali built a blazing fire in his durbar,
To pray to the Gods to become the mightiest of all,
Into the congregation walked a tiny, tiny man.
Asked Bali, "Who are you, you seem rather small?"

"Don't be fooled by my size," said the little man,
"I may be small O King but I am not meek.
I have come today to ask you for something
With the hope that I will get what I seek."

Bali arose and said, "Please be my guest,
What can I do for you? What is it you desire?"
"Oh not much," said the man, "Just a bit of land,
Only as much as three of my steps can acquire."

Surprised, Bali said, "That's a strange request.
Why not ask for bigger gifts: for silver or for gold?"
"The greatest treasures are often small," said the man,
"I shall be glad with the land my three steps can hold!"

"Well, so be it," said Bali, "take your three steps!"
Smiling mysteriously, the man put one foot ahead.
Then something strange occurred, for the little man
Began to grow and grow, and spread and spread!

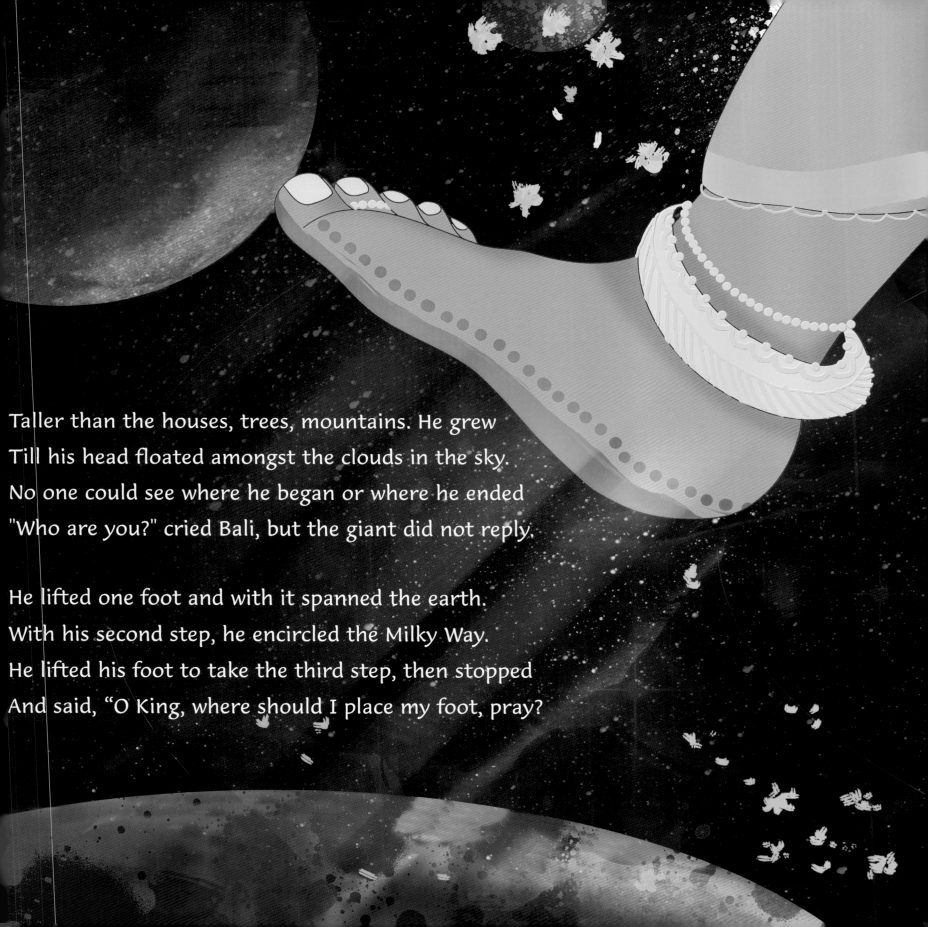

Taller than the houses, trees, mountains. He grew
Till his head floated amongst the clouds in the sky.
No one could see where he began or where he ended
"Who are you?" cried Bali, but the giant did not reply.

He lifted one foot and with it spanned the earth.
With his second step, he encircled the Milky Way.
He lifted his foot to take the third step, then stopped
And said, "O King, where should I place my foot, pray?

I hope you will not go back on your word;
You did promise me three steps, didn't you?"
By now Bali had guessed who the giant was:
None other than the supreme Lord Vishnu.

"Greed and arrogance had blinded me O Lord.
Foolish I may be but a liar I am not," Bali said.
"Please place your third step here," he entreated,
As he removed his crown and lowered his head.

Vishnu was pleased to see the king repent.
"Good you have realized your folly," he said.
"Ask for what will make you truly happy;
Let me now grant you a wish instead."

"I have only one desire now O Lord," said Bali.
"Please live here, spend a few days with me.
It will give me the chance to make amends;
I do hope you will accept my humble plea."

Vishnu agreed and stayed on in Bali's palace,
But Lakshmi, Vishnu's wife, missed him dearly.
Yearning to see her husband who had left long ago,
She set off alone for Bali's kingdom eagerly.

Bali welcomed Lakshmi into his home with joy.
"I have come here as your sister," Lakshmi said.
"I have a wish that I hope you will fulfil, O King."
Saying this, on Bali's wrist she tied a silk thread.

Touched, Bali said: "Ask me what you want!"
"I have come for my husband," said Lakshmi.
"Accept my apology, my sister," repented Bali.
"I have been selfish to make him stay with me."

Lakshmi happily returned home with her husband,
Bali lost his Lord, but a valuable lesson he did learn:
Life's real treasures are not our possessions, but
What we do for each other and the love we earn

"I like this story!," said Klaka, mesmerized
"We want more, more!," cried the other two,
"Well you are in luck today," said Amma,
"For I have two more stories for you!

Once the heavens", continued Amma,
"Were attacked by a mighty demon band.
Indra led the Gods into fearsome battle
But, the demons gained the upper hand.

On seeing this, Indra's wife Saachi panicked.
She wanted Indra to be victorious in the fight
And rushed to a wise sage to seek his advice,
He said, "Tie a thread on Indra's wrist tonight."

That evening after a long and weary battle,
Saachi tended to Indra, nursing each injury.
She lovingly tied a silk thread on his wrist, saying
"May you win, Indra, may you achieve victory."

The next day, Indra emerged on the battlefield
With his vigour renewed and strength restored.
His troops were enthused and rallied behind him;
They fought together and finally won the war!"

"How can a thread help you win a war?" asked Klaka.
Amma said, "Well, the thread does nothing by itself.
It is the love of the person who ties it, that gives you
The strength to persevere and believe in yourself!

And now for the last story of the day," said Amma.
"No, no! We want more, more!" protested all three.
Smiling, Amma added: "This one is from the year 1905,
When Britain ruled over India and we were not free.

The British decided to divide the state of Bengal in two,
Separating Hindus from Muslims, making them fight.
Rabindranath Tagore, the famous thinker, poet, writer,
Had an idea by which the two communities could unite.

The festival of Raksha Bandhan was around the corner,
Tagore urged Hindus and Muslims to celebrate together.
To honour his plea, throngs from both communities
Tied rakhis as symbols of love and peace to each other.

Bonds between Hindus and Muslims strengthened.
Together, they challenged the move to divide the state.
Ultimately, the British had no choice but to concede;
Bengal was reunited then, it was a time to celebrate.

Tagore showed us what Raksha Bandhan truly is,"
Said Amma, "to fearlessly stand up for each other;
It is our responsibility to protect all those around us,
Be it parent, friend, neighbour, sister or brother!

So my dear Maya, Klaka and Kiki, I do hope
That you will forever celebrate this day together.
And will always love and be there for each other,
During sunny days as well as stormy weather."

Glossary

Amma: mother

Diya: a clay lamp with a cotton wick dipped in oil

Hanuman: the popular Hindu deity and one of the central characters in the epic Ramayana - an ardent devotee of Rama and a general of the mythical Vanara tribe of beings that are half human and half ape

Indra: god of heavens and of lightning in Hinduism

Krishna: an avatar of Vishnu; the central character in the epic Mahabharata and the narrator of the 'Bhagvad Gita'

Kumkum: a red powder made from turmeric and slaked lime

Laddu: a ball-shaped sweet made of flour, milk and sugar, often served at festive occasions

Rabindranath Tagore: (May 7, 1861 to Aug 7, 1941) a poet, philosopher, writer, film maker and music composer from the state of Bengal; Winner of Nobel Prize in Literature in 1913, the first Asian recipient of the prize

Tilak: the Hindu ritual of marking a person's forehead with a fragrant paste, such as sandalwood or kumkum, as a mark of love and respect

Vishnu: the Hindu God, tasked with protecting the Universe

The 'Amma Take Me' Series: Come Explore The Places Where We Worship!

This new series, published under Puffin Books by Penguin Random House India, introduces readers to the history of the major Indian faiths through their important places of worship. Styled as travelogues of a mother and her two young children, told in a fun and engaging way, these books link history, tradition and mythology to bring alive the monuments. The books are for children in the 8 to 12 year age group.

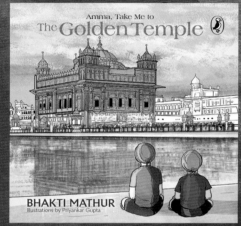

Amma, Take Me to
The Golden Temple

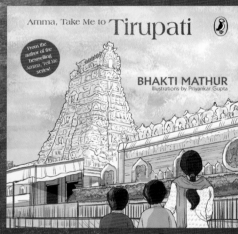

Amma, Take Me to Tirupati

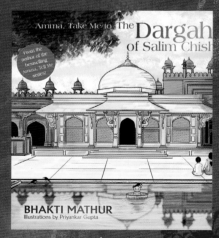

Amma, Take Me to The
Dargah of Salim Chishti

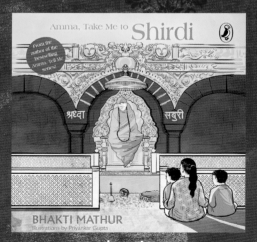

Amma, Take Me to Shirdi

Books available on Amazon India and Amazon US.